THE RULES OF
MODERN
POLICING

1973 EDITION

This book belongs to

DC Chris Skelton
(black belt trained)

so get off it or i'll hunt you
down and karate chop your
bloody head.

I could do it too. Easy.

The Mothership – North-West Division's head offices.

THE RULES OF
MODERN
POLICING

1973 EDITION

DCI GENE HUNT

BANTAM PRESS

LONDON · NEW YORK · TORONTO · SYDNEY · AUCKLAND

TRANSWORLD PUBLISHERS
61–63 Uxbridge Road, London W5 5SA
A Random House Group Company
www.rbooks.co.uk

First published in Great Britain in 2007 by Bantam Press
an imprint of Transworld Publishers

A CIP catalogue record for this book is available from the British Library.

ISBN 9780593060209

Writer: Guy Adams
Designer: Lee Thompson
Commissioning Editor: Sarah Emsley
Editorial Angel: Rebecca Jones

Addresses for Random House Group Ltd companies outside
the UK can be found at: www.randomhouse.co.uk
The Random House Group Ltd Reg. No. 954009

The Random House Group Ltd makes every effort to ensure that the papers
used in its books are made from trees that have been legally sourced from
well-managed and credibly certified forests. Our paper procurement policy
can be found at: www.randomhouse.co.uk/paper.htm

Typeset in Baskerville & BigBlox
Printed and bound in Great Britain by
Butler & Tanner, Frome

4 6 8 10 9 7 5

www.kudosfilmandtv.com
www.bbc.co.uk/lifeonmars

Table of Contents

Introduction   7

1 Equipment   9

2 Cars and Driving   17

3 Understanding Criminals   27

4 Conducting an Investigation   37

5 Vice   67

6 Interrogating Suspects   75

7 Staff Relations   95

8 Off Duty   105

9 External Relations and Complaints   113

Appendix One Looking the Part   116

Appendix Two Simple Advice for Plod   119

Appendix Three Glossary   122

The Guv.

Introduction

Sit down, shut up and pay attention.

The powers that be – recognising a genius copper
when they see one – have asked me to lay down
the basic rules I teach my division to keep the soft
sacks out of trouble and on the ball.

Modern policing is a tricky business and it takes
more than they teach you at plod school to do the
job. It's dangerous. Being a copper these days is
like brushing a lion's teeth with your tadger…
risky and only for those with balls of steel.

Like me.

So read…learn…and, if you're lucky, some of it
might rub off.

Gene Hunt

DCI Gene Hunt
Spring, 1973

1 Equipment

You can never be completely prepared for police work (otherwise we could all go home and leave it to the boy scouts). Still, there's a few basic bits of kit that come in handy so often it would be stupid not to shove them in a pocket or the boot of your motor.

From the sort of things every bloke needs to get through life with a smile on his gob, to more specialised equipment you can break out of police stores (or your local ironmongers), here's Gene's shopping list:

Fig. 1.1.a Brain Catalyst Dispenser – the hip flask.

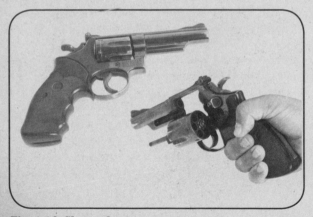

Fig. 1.1.b Sharp shooters.

1.1 Tools of the Trade

At times you'll have to play this by ear – certain situations will require specialist equipment. Example: If you're dealing with the big boys and signing out the shooters, then for Christ's sake get a bloody cannon on your hip – last thing you want is to go into a potential shoot-out with a pop gun in your hand. If it looks like it would have an elephant's kneecap off, chances are nobody's going to force you to pull the trigger.

Still, there are some things you will need every day and should never leave home without:

a. **Hip flask.** We all know there's only one way of really clearing the head in the morning after an evening of quiet relaxation at the pub, and that's 'hair of the dog' (and no, I'm not talking about the missus' wig). A quick shot of something warming sets you up for the day, especially if followed by a bacon butty. Single malt and pig grease: the oil that keeps the detection engine running.

(c)

BRUT

(b)

b. **Fags.** Keep the lungs clear of exhaust
    fumes and show you're a decent bloke
    when you offer them round. Nothing sets
    an informant at ease more than bunging
    him a Rothmans (even if you do knock it
    out of his gob the minute he tells a porkie
    – all part of the game).

c. **Bottle of Brut** (or similar). Keeps the flies
    off and the birds on.

d. **Pack of cards.** Not only can they help to
    pass the time but they can also pad out
    the wallet nicely, too.

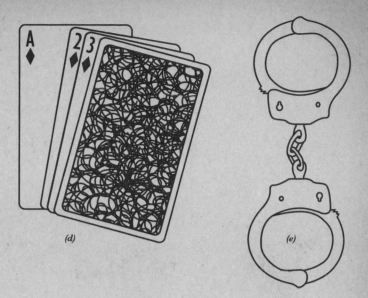

(d)

(e)

e. <u>**Cuffs**</u>. Sounds obvious but you'd be surprised how many times I've seen an officer caught short of the bracelets. Not only are they a vital piece of equipment for keeping Johnny Slag trussed up and out of trouble, some of you might find a use for them at home as well. Know what I mean?

f. Don't forget to pack something heavy and blunt in the car boot either. There's nothing quite as good as a <u>**crowbar**</u> for opening doors and closing mouths.

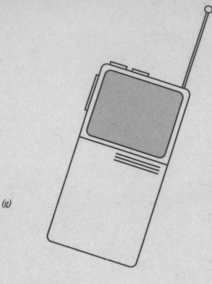

(g)

g.   **<u>Radio</u>**. You can't be out and about and
     cut off from home, can you? An essential
     piece of police equipment for picking the
     best jobs, calling back-up and keeping
     your ear on the football score.

h.   Last but not least, always keep a bit of
     <u>cash</u> on the hip. How else are you going
     to keep informants talking or stand your
     round if you've only a few pennies in your
     pocket?

Test Yourself on This Section

Time to find out if you've been paying attention! All very well you flicking through this book and admiring the handsome bastard in the photos, but if you don't learn from it then we'll all have been wasting our time, won't we?

1. What is the best calibre bullet to carry if involved in a shoot-out?
   a. 9 mm ✗
   b. 0.22 inch (long rifle) ✓
   c. 0.38 inch ✗
   d. 0.45 inch ✗

2. If you could take only two items with you when out on the streets, which would you choose?
   a. Hip flask and fags. ✗
   b. Feather duster and handcuffs. ✗
   c. Deck of cards and a crowbar. ✓
   d. Notebook and pen. ✗

3. Why is it vital to keep your car on the radio?
   a. So you don't miss *The Archers*. ✗
   b. So you can keep in touch with Control. ✓
   c. So you can tune in to *Pick of the Pops*. ✗
   d. So you know when your shift's finished. ✗

ANSWERS

1. If you answered...

a. You're a pansy – a dead one probably.

b. You think you're hunting bunnies, you twonk.

c. You're using standard police ammunition, good boy.

d. You think you're Dirty Harry. Can I have a go?

2. If you answered...

a. You're a sensible man, give us a light.

b. You're a kinky bastard. *learned from the best!*

c. You're a nutter.

d. You're a constable – go and watch traffic.

3. If you answered...

a. You should be deaf. *YES!!!*

b. You're 'tuned in'.

c. You're Alan Freeman and if I can think of a sound legal reason to have you I will.

d. You're Uniform.

2 Cars and Driving

hello! send in Skelton!

Never underestimate the importance of your car.
Not only does it get you from A to B but at times it
will be your bedroom, your office and the greasy
spoon you eat your breakfast in of a morning.
Your car also shows your status; you see me pull
up in my Mark III Cortina and you immediately
think I'm the business, don't you? A man of taste,
discernment with a manhood of such size it's a
wonder I fit it under the dashboard.

2.1 The Perfect Motor

Beautiful, isn't she? Goes like sugar off a shovel and holds the road like shit to a blanket.

There is no better car for pursuit either; I push the pedal on this and the vibration alone could make a nun cum. This thing has thicker carpets than your front room and more wood than Sherwood Forest.

Learn all of the following and maybe one day you'll deserve to own one.

**Ford Cortina
Mark III 2000E**

SPECIFICATIONS	
Engine	*In-line 1993cc 4 cylinder ohc (rocket)*
Bore x stroke	*90.82 x 76.95mm*
Maximum power	*105bhp @ 5500prm*
Transmission	*4 speed*
Wheelbase	*101.5in (2580mm)*
Wheels	*Fast*
Track	*65.9in (1445mm)*
Length	*167.7in (4260mm)*
Front suspension	*SLA coil and wishbone*
Rear suspension	*Beam axle with upper/lower trailing arms and coil springs*
Brakes	*Four-wheel hydraulic (front disc/rear drum)*
Maximum speed	*PDQ*

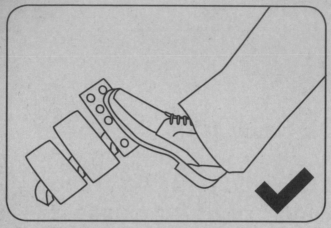

Fig. 2.2.a Good Pedal Action.

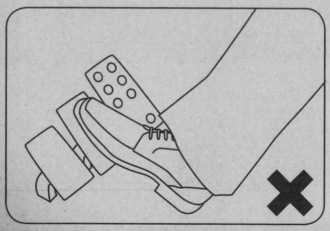

Fig. 2.2.b Poor Pedal Action. It'll get you nowhere.

2.2 The My Way Code

However good your motor, it's no use unless you know how to drive it. Here are some basic pointers for good road use:

a. Does Graham Hill try for second place? No, he bloody doesn't and neither should you. Put your foot down and give 'er welly. They wouldn't have given you a clock that goes up to 120 if they didn't want you to use some of it, would they?

b. Don't get too happy with your brake foot. A footbrake is a necessary evil – a good driver knows to use it sparingly and at the last minute. The truly advanced driver keeps an eye out for street furniture to help with sudden stops, too. Bins are a particular favourite – they're light enough not to cause significant paintwork problems but noisy enough to let people know you've arrived. The handbrake's for turning and parking (especially turning).

c. Streets and alleyways have been carefully laid out with traffic lights, one-way systems and pedestrian access just so that you can get where you need to go quickly without other drivers getting under your feet. Keep your eyes peeled, your foot down and your warrant card to hand so the traffic boys know who they're turning a blind eye to.

Fig. 2.2.c Giving it welly.

d.   I have noticed certain officers wearing their seat belt while driving. This not only messes up your nice suit (see Appendix One), it also restricts your movement behind the wheel. Very dangerous.

e.   One of the main dangers a good driver faces is those silly bastards on foot: pedestrians. They get in the way and, if you're not careful, can lead to accidents. Combining the horn with some good roaring revs usually warns them to get their backs against the wall. But watch out – nobody wants to lose a pursuit because they're too busy washing a granny off the windshield.

Fig. 2.2.d Lots of wood.

f.   Don't be too smart getting into your motor. Sliding over the bonnet may sound flash but you won't be the first to look a tosser when you tear your windscreen wipers off and end up on your face somewhere near the front wheel. Walk to the door, open the door, get in the car. Not difficult, is it?

g.   I'm a big believer in the driving glove. A swanky pair of stringbacks gives you increased grip on the wheel and also look great. (They can protect your knuckles a little in a fight, too.)

h. Hang one of those Magic Tree air fresheners off your rear-view mirror and you'll see how quickly I can make you swallow it. Christ, you may as well just put a frock on and start ballet dancing, you big girl. Open the window if the thick musk of real men bothers you.

girls love policeman musk

Test Yourself on This Section

Now then, sharpen your pencil again and slip your brain into fourth...

1. Which is the best speed range for the police driver?
   a. 0–20 mph ✗
   b. 20–40 mph ✗
   c. 40–80 mph ✓
   d. 80–120 mph ✗

2. What is the purpose of a one-way system?
   a. To encourage a sensible level of traffic in the city centre. ✗
   b. To help lady drivers who get scared if they see something coming towards them. ✓
   c. To give the police driver better options for navigation while in pursuit. ✗
   d. To cause accidents. ✗

3. The smell of sweaty blokes in your motor is getting strong. Should you...
   a. Hang a Magic Tree air freshener from your rear-view mirror. ✗
   b. Ask everyone to wear more aftershave. ✗
   c. Hold your hand over your nose and start whinging. ✗
   d. Suck it in and thank God that you're a man in good company. ✓

ANSWERS

1. If you answered...

    a.   *You should get a push-bike, you're a waste of tarmac space.*

    b.   *You're a pensioner and are probably in my way...MOVE!!!!*

    c.   *You're in my passenger seat and loving it.* **Vroom Vroom!**

    d.   *You're insane but I'd love to watch (from a safe distance).*

2. If you answered...

    a.   *You're a boring git who believes everything the papers tell you.*

    b.   *You're my wife.* **No I m bloody not!**

    c.   *You're a man after my own heart.*

    d.   *You're a bloody liability.*

3. If you answered...

    a.   *You're a poof.*

    b.   *You're a poof.*

    c.   *You're a poof.*

    d.   *You're a good bloke (or a poof and getting excited).*

        Good bloke. Definitely.

3 Understanding Criminals

There's a lot of talk creeping in these days about the need to understand the criminal's mind.

Now, this is important but what worries me is the hand-holding and talk of motivation that seems to go along with it. We need to understand these blaggers so that we can catch them, not give them a big hug and invite them to our mum's for tea.

Still, for those who insist on a bit of science...

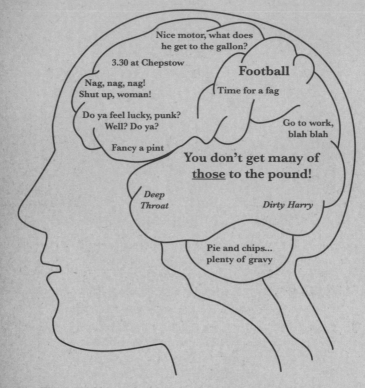

Fig. 3.1.1 Normal man's brain.

3.1 Basic Biology

Here's a look at the normal bloke's mind (*Fig. 3.1.1*). Nothing surprising, just the stuff that bubbles up all the time:

Shall I have a fag? Or maybe go for a pint…What's for tea tonight and will the missus go on and on and on…? Of course she will, her mouth's as saggy as her knickers and when was the last time she bothered to let me have a go on…Bloody hell! Look at that! She wouldn't drown at sea, would she? Not bad from behind either…

These are the normal, healthy thoughts of a red-blooded man, a bloke brought up on a sensible diet of beer, curry, John Wayne and *Jugs Digest*. It's certainly what's going through my head most of the time. If it's not what's going through yours then I reckon this book's as much use to you as a wank mag to the Pope. Still, it's not necessarily what goes through the mind of a criminal, as we shall see…

Let's take a look at the brain of a blagger:

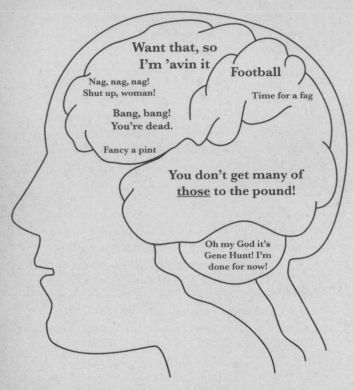

Fig. 3.1.2 Blagger's brain.

He may still have a nagging wife and a healthy respect for skirt (blagger or not, he's still a bloke), but there's a number of all-important differences...

3.2 The Differences

The trick to understanding and dealing with criminals lies in those obvious differences between them and us. If you accept these differences and work with them they can be your best guide to putting a stop to the sods.

a. Blaggers go out and take whatever they want rather than work to earn it. But that's OK – once you know what they want you can plan ahead, can't you? Say you're dealing with a gang of bank robbers…You don't start keeping your eye on florists, do you? Stake out the banks!

b. Some of them don't give a tinker's tadger about anyone who stands in their way. So, bear that in mind and get ready to duck.

c. They're scared of **you**. Of course they are, they don't want to get caught. When you're scared you make mistakes, so encourage 'em. Make it known through your snouts or, God help us, the press that you're getting closer and when you catch 'em their knackers will have as much chance of getting out intact as a fat lass on an island full of cannibals. Feed their fear!

d.   They're not as imaginative as you. You spend your time hopping from one case to another, thinking creatively. They do what they do and that's it. You find that most criminals stick to what they know: they rob banks and post offices, they deal drugs, they fence goods…Their limitations will always give you an advantage.

These basic points extend to most 'career criminals'. Things get tricky when you start getting into the sewer that is the mind of a nutjob killer or a rapist:

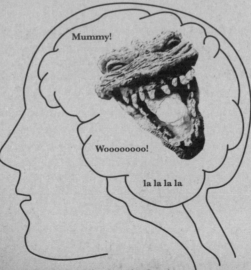

Fig. 3.2.1 Nutjob killer/rapist brain.

See? Madder than eels in a bowl of tapioca and that's a fact.

Still, at the end of the day there's one piece of science that's reassuring. Hit 'em hard enough and all brains look like *Fig. 3.2.2*.

So let's not worry, eh?

Right, enough of the *Tomorrow's World* stuff.

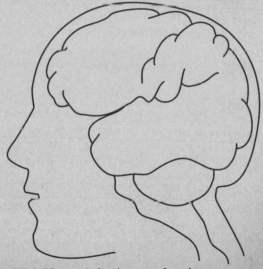

Fig. 3.2.2 Blagger's brain, post-beating.

Test Yourself on This Section

Understand the mind of a criminal? Let's find out:

1. How do most of us get what we want in life?
    a. Go to work, earn a living and buy things with
        our hard-earned cash. ✓
    b. Whack someone in the face over and over until
        they give it to you. ✗
    c. Ask your mummy nicely if Father Christmas
        will bring it this year. ✗
    d. I don't know, I've always had everything I
        want. ✗

2. What are the two main things a criminal has that
    will help you catch him?
    a. A stripy jumper and a bag with 'swag' written
        on it in big black letters (*Fig. 2.a*). ✗
    b. Fear and a lack of imagination (*Fig. 2.b*). ✓
    c. A big gun and the urge to shoot you with it.
        (*Fig. 2.c*). ✗
    d. A nice car and wonderful dress sense.
        (*Fig. 2.d*). ✗

3. When faced with a psycho loony what should you do?
    a. Talk to him and try to 'relate' to his
        problems. ✗
    b. Sit down and go through his collection of body
        parts over a cup of tea and a biscuit. ✗
    c. Hit him repeatedly with something blunt until
        he stops trying to kill you. ✓
    d. Run away like a big pansy in a ballet skirt. ✗

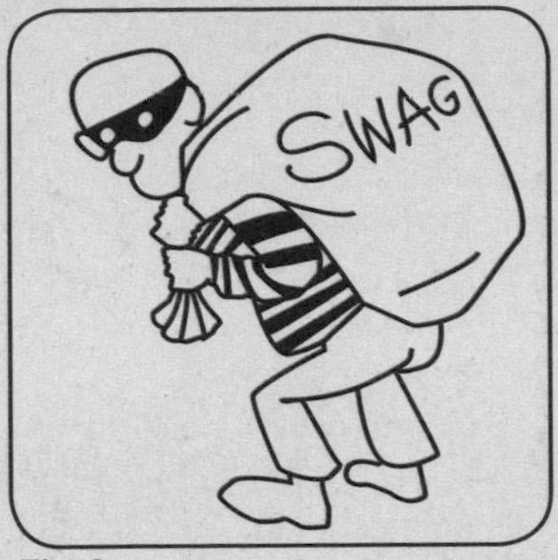

Aaagh! Save me from Skelton!

Fig. 2.a

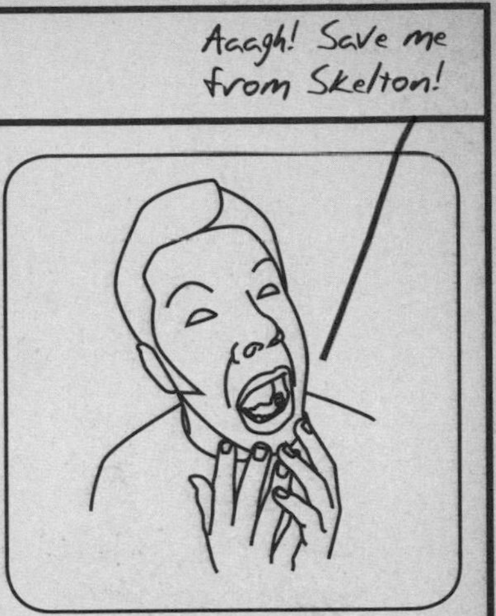

Fig. 2.b

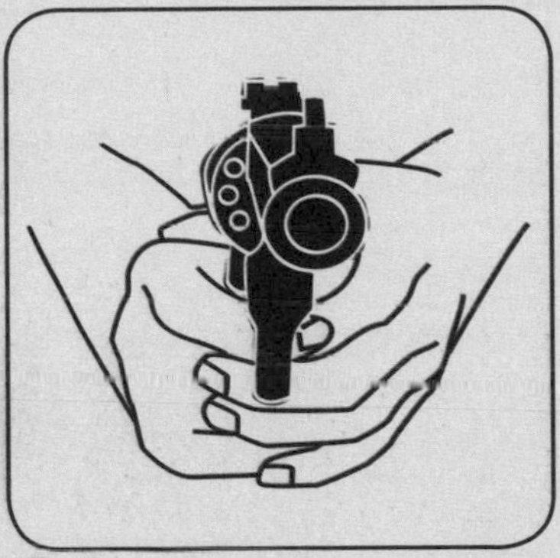

Fig. 2.c

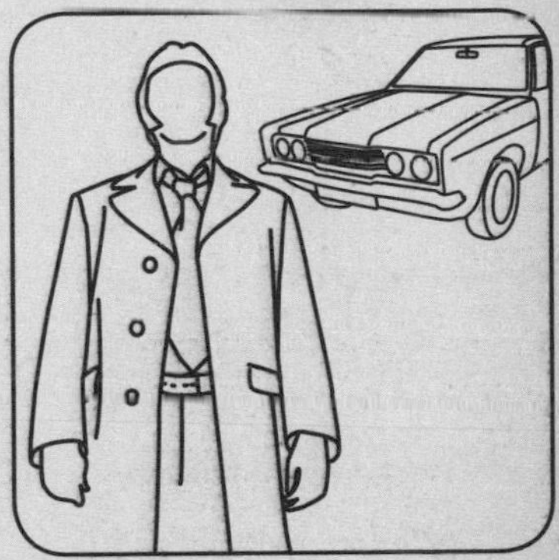

Fig. 2.d

ANSWERS

1. If you answered...

a. You're a normal bloke. *Damn right!*

b. You're a crook and I'm on my way to nab you.

c. You're embarrassing me now, stop it.

d. You're the Chief Inspector. Hello, Chief Inspector.

2. If you answered...

a. You're an idiot.

b. You're paying attention. *Yeah!!*

c. You've got a death wish.

d. You're thinking about me again. Understandable but try to concentrate.

3. If you answered...

a. You're a ponce – hope he bites your face off.

b. You're as bad as he is. Stop looking at me like that.

c. You beat me to it. Well played.

d. You're a big pansy in a ballet skirt, obviously.

Full marks to Professor Skelton – Cheif Criminologest!!!

4 Conducting an Investigation

If you cast your mind back to your school science lessons you may remember – alongside fannying about with Bunsen burners and snapping the bra strap of the girl in front – the phrase 'path of least resistance'. Police work is a lot like that – you've a job to do, a cell to fill, now all you need to do is figure out the quickest way to do it.

Now I'm not saying you ignore the law governing officers in the line of work, I'm just making the point that police work requires you to have an open mind. Sometimes the best way is not always the most obvious way, and it's your duty to keep on your toes and feel your way through the mess, the paperwork, the lies and the laws.

Fig. 4.1.1 Filling his brain with big words, getting nowhere.

Fig. 4.1.2 Getting the job done!

4.1 Rules of Thumb

Police work is creative and no one rule will always apply.

Having said that, here are a few general Golden Greats that have worked well for me:

a.   At a crime scene you're going to hear a lot of opinion, a lot of misunderstanding and a lot of guff from witnesses. <u>Remember the all-important rule of crowd chat: the first one to speak did it.</u> They can't keep their gobs shut – desperate to sound innocent, they put their foot in it and do the opposite.

b.   The hunch is the copper's friend. The gut knows more than the brain ever will. <u>Don't dismiss a hunch just because the facts don't fit; keep digging and they soon will.</u> Even when we were cavemen braining one another with clubs for nicking our mammoth steaks we relied on instinct to point us in the right direction when knowledge fails. <u>Never let your head rule your gut.</u>

c. **<u>Don't ignore the obvious.</u>** Too many coppers try and make life complicated. If you're called to a house where a woman is lying dead in a bed with a naked milkman on top of her and nobody's seen the husband for two days, we can safely say this is not a crime about the price of dairy produce. Don't go all Agatha Christie about things. More often than not it's the simple solution that's the right one.

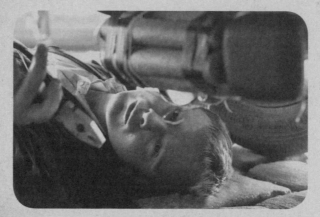

Fig. 4.1.c If it looks like a bomb and ticks like a bomb, it's highly likely that what you're looking at is a bloody great bomb.

4.2 The Crime Scene

Crimes aren't solved by poncing around the desk moving sheets of paper, you need to get out on to the streets and get the ball rolling. First stop, the crime scene:

a.   Nobody likes watching the flies at a murder scene, puts you right off your breakfast. Still, got to be done. Get a fag in your mouth to keep the smell off and get in there.

That's me!!!!!

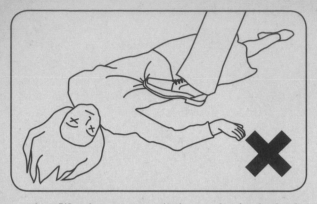

b. Watch your step. A size twelve in the body cavity doesn't help the coroner's job.

c. Have a strong stomach on camera duty. If some delicate fairy loses his lunch over the evidence, everyone's got sticky fingers trying to sort it out.

d.   Put on a show. Chances are you'll have the
     press and public wandering about. Give
     'em nothing to go on, but look like you're
     on top of the situation (even if you haven't
     a bloody clue).

e.   Avoid getting caught in front of a press
     microphone. The bastards will only make
     you look a div on the evening news and it
     would be suicide to start giving opinion at
     this stage in the game.

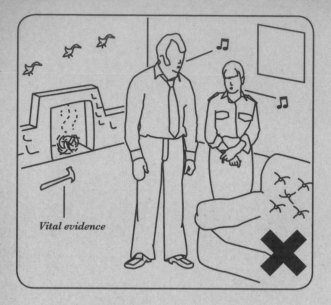

Vital evidence

f.   Keep 'em peeled. We all know that a
     crime scene is filled with little details
     – bits of evidence, important clues. Get
     Plod doing a sweep if you like – looks
     good and keeps them out of trouble.

Harriet Ambrose (Plonk – SD246)
        Sheffield 2012

4.3 Gathering Information

While combing the crime scene and getting the lab boys to check for dabs – the gathering of physical evidence – is a good start, sooner or later you're going to have to start talking to people so you can put all your information in context.

    a.   First step in a murder inquiry is to **drag in everyone the stiff knew** – especially the wife or husband. Sod the butler, this is Manchester, the spouse always did it. Even if it's not a murder you need to start filling the canteen with bodies that might know something. Set the girls chatting with staff, witnesses…anyone within spitting distance of the crime scene. Plonk likes to talk – does it ever stop?

    b.   **Informants.** Every DCI worth his badge needs a few people he can call on who have their ears to the ground and greedy enough pockets to share what they know. This is also where an officer knows to play the long game – don't go nicking everyone with criminal connections, let the little fish keep swimming for a while. They pay for their freedom by making sure they keep you on track with the big boys.

You seen this bird?

c. **<u>Door to Door.</u>** Marching up and down the streets like a double-glazing salesman. God help you but it has to be done. The thing to remember is that 90 per cent of what anyone tells you is bollocks. You have to see through the confusion, assumption and stupidity if you want to know the important facts.

4.4 Using the Press to Your Advantage

OK, so we all hate the newspapers. Beyond checking the form of either Aintree or page three, they're filled with pointless drivel and, more often than not, set out to cause problems for the Force. Still, sometimes they do have their uses...

    a.   Pour enough Scotch down a journalist's throat and you might just find out a few things. The press do have access to information that we don't (we move in gutter circles, but compared to the ones hacks move in it's a Royal Garden Party; a rat would wash its gob after biting a journo).

Fig. 4.4.a Our local rag with some highly distressing news that caused tears in our office.

b. In 3.2.c I mentioned using criminals' fear against them. Telling the papers that you're close to catching a suspect is a good way of doing that. Makes you look good and gets the blaggers hot under the collar.

c. Sometimes you might have a photo (or, God help us, a police sketch*) that you can release to the press. It's a good way of getting that information into as many hands as possible but bear in mind you may as well be placing an advert saying: 'Please could all timewasters and lunatics contact their local police station as officers really fancy having so much cobblers thrown at them that they would happily ram pencils in their ears rather than sit through another word.'

* I've seen blind men draw better than most sketch artists. Seriously, I once had thirty or forty phone calls trying to shop Roger Whittaker for a murder in Levenshulme. I'd have nabbed him for a laugh but we were looking for a woman for Christ's sake.

Fig. 4.4.c A 'helpful' sketch of a teenage boy wanted for arson.

4.5 The Stakeout

The stakeout is a horrible part of policing life. Sweaty coppers bundled into a car for hours on end until just opening your gob in the car is as foul as licking the concrete in a monkey house. Not nice. Still, there are a few things that can make life easier:

a. <u>**A good takeaway.**</u> All right, so it stinks the car out even more but which would you rather be smelling – a DI's armpits or stale vindaloo?

b. <u>**Some light refreshment.**</u> Keep your hip flask handy. Note: avoid beer. I had a particularly unpleasant night a couple of years ago – four officers, a crate of beer and no toilet close by. An empty R. White's bottle only goes so far...

c. As tempting as it may be, <u>keep the</u> <u>cards in your pocket.</u> You don't want your suspect wandering off while you're chasing a full house. The first one to suggest I-spy gets shot...

d. <u>Keep your eye on the ball</u>, even if the big girl at number 42 has forgotten to draw the curtains before having a bath.*

e. The most important rule of a stakeout – <u>do your best not to get chosen for it!</u>

---

* Of course it's times like this when rank plays an important part. Flash your stripes and get somebody else to watch the suspect while you watch the loofah action to your heart's content.

4.6 Going Undercover

Probably the most dangerous area of the job. This isn't doing a turn in your school play, your mummy ain't going to be giving you a round of applause and a peck on the cheek for remembering your lines.

You're Brando, Pacino…Gary Cooper. You're on your own, and you need to fit in.

Mind you, the perks can be good – the wife has my time as a member of Harry Stoke's gang to thank for the colour telly in our front room.* Swings and roundabouts, eh?

Going undercover can be split into two subsections: impersonating a target and impersonating a criminal…

* Well, the evidence room was getting a bit full, wasn't it? Just trying to do my best to help keep the place straight. Besides, anything that helps to keep Mrs Hunt's trap shut is a good thing for all of Manchester.

4.6 ½ Impersonating a Target

a. When it comes to costume **don't get too carried away.** I had a DS once who was pretending to be a postman after a spate of mail thefts. He turned up with a false moustache that looked like Barbara Cartland's fanny and a hunchback that kept slipping. Twonk thought he was Peter Sellers. The idea is to blend in, **not** stand out a mile.

b. **Keep your head down.** As above, you're supposed to be part of the background. For example, if you and a bunch of other officers are pretending to be staff in a bank that your genius of a Guv reckons is in line for a hold-up, just quietly go about your business, **don't draw suspicion.** Karate-chopping every bastard that comes through the doors or wafting chunks of cash around shouting, 'Ooh, anybody want some?' is unlikely to end in the arrest of anyone but yourself.

Claire (Big Tits, Brown Hair)
Hill Valley 2015

Fig. 4.6½.a Not ideal for undercover work with criminals, Tufty being a kids' mascot and all.

cheer up, guv

Fig. 4.6½.b *Perfect for undercover work, especially in a pub. If you're not in a pub, ditch the towel. Flexible.*

c. <u>**We don't want any heroes.**</u> Undercover operations are dangerous and carefully controlled. The last thing anybody needs is some tit thinking he's John Wayne and trying to take everybody on before the word's gone out. You'll end up deader than a cat in a Chinese restaurant, and probably take half your team with you.

d. If the worst comes to the worst and you end up as a hostage, then it's even more important you <u>**keep your cover.**</u> Announcing to a bunch of desperate criminals that you're a copper is about as clever as Mickey Mouse turning up to Top Cat's birthday party with a pilchard up his arse. Keep your gob shut unless you want someone to put their boot into it.

Mouse guts!!

4.6 ¾ Impersonating a Criminal

a. <u>**Knowledge and experience is vital.**</u> You can't pass for a member of a gang of armed robbers if the first thing you do when picking up a shotgun is blow your own foot off. You need to look as if you belong. Stands to reason too that you shouldn't over-exaggerate your abilities. It's all very well you putting it about that you're the best safe-cracker around so that you'll get yourself 'hired' by a gang, but when you're called to prove it you're going to look a right arse sat there with a hammer and a stethoscope getting nowhere.

b. <u>**Know the lingo.**</u> It's no good shoving one of those bloody university lot in, is it? Have them simpering around talking about 'ruffians' and 'peelers' like they're straight off *The Lavender Hill Mob*. You need someone whose background and accent makes him fit in.

c. **<u>Don't lose perspective.</u>** Yeah, you have to fit in, you have to get on with the criminals you're mixing with, but just remember when you start having a laugh over a pint that you're going to be nicking him at any moment. By all means, share a bag of pork scratchings with 'em…just don't get too pally.

d. **<u>Know your limits and be ready to walk away.</u>** Nobody wants to blow a case because you dropped out, but you have to read the way things are going. If you think for one minute they're on to you then vanish. You're not helping anyone by hanging around. Also, what if things turn nasty and you're expected to prove yourself to the crooks? Nicking a few odds and sods in the name of the law's one thing but are you going to pull the trigger on a civilian if asked?*

*Depends who it is, granted. Traffic warden, journalist, politician or Rolf Harris, then blow their bloody brains out…Otherwise you're in trouble, pal.

4.7 Interpreting the Law

In the old days the law was rigid; now times are more enlightened.

We have the responsibility and privilege of being encouraged to 'interpret' the law. This means that it becomes whatever you need it to be at the time. If you know a man's guilty all your efforts need to be aimed towards proving that. By which, of course, I actually mean you have to 'make it stick in a court of law', which isn't always the same thing from their point of view.

For example, the other day I turned over a suspected thief's flat and found a spare room filled with hot radios. Job done. Now we all know that a detective needs justifiable cause to search a suspect's house. My justifiable cause? Well, I could have sworn I smelled gas outside his front door...just acting in the best interests of the other tenants' safety, wasn't I? Progress, you've got to love it.

The law's not just your job, it's your friend!

Never fit up anyone who doesn't deserve it.

4.8 Making an Arrest

Assuming you follow all of the above, you might even get to the position of making an arrest!

That is, after all, the bloody point.

You would think, having managed to get this far, that I wouldn't need to give you any advice on this one.

But I'm not jumping to conclusions as some of the arrest procedures I've seen in my time are enough to make me want to put myself in solitary confinement just to get away from you silly bastards.

So…basic, obvious pointers:

a. **Don't** shout 'You're under arrest!' from fifty feet away. This is the most common cock-up in arrest procedure. I can only assume the silly gobshites that do this every damn time love both the sound of their own voice and chasing the slag they've just given a sound head start to for half an hour. Subtlety, girls, saves the shoe leather.

Fig. 4.8.1 Note the look of fear on his face; he knows what's coming.

Fig. 4.8.2 Classic arm position; he'll be eating grass for as long as you want.

b. **Do** cuff 'em. Don't laugh, I've seen it. Gormless pair of CID with a combined intelligence of a cat's fart wondering why their cheeks hurt and they're lying on their backs beside a car completely empty of suspects.

Fig. 4.8.3 Another one banged up – time for a pint!

c. **<u>Do</u>** put them in the back seat with someone to hold their hand for them in case they get scared. I don't care if they say they get car sick. You don't want a desperate criminal sitting up front with the driver – they will be tempted to get up to all sorts of bad behaviour – and I don't mean fiddling with the radio station or getting fag ash on the upholstery. You try driving straight when you've got a crazed skinhead hanging off your earlobe by his teeth…These boys get frisky when caught, I'm telling you.

d. **<u>Do</u>** learn to ignore the bullshit. On your way to the station you will hear enough stories to give Enid Blyton a run for her money. He needs the lav, he needs fresh air, he needs his medication…What he needs is a gentle slap to the gob and to learn to appreciate the pleasure of silence. Just get him through the station door and worry about what he needs after he's under lock and key.

Test Yourself on This Section

A bumper selection for a bumper section. Don't go thinking I'd let you get away with it too easily!

1. You're called to a crime scene at the circus. The lion tamer is lying dead next to a brightly painted clown's car with 'Coco is a twat' written all over it. The man died by being kicked to death by size 24 shoes. Who is the most likely suspect?
   a. The butler. ✗
   b. Ernst Stavro Blofeld. ✗
   c. Moriarty. ✗
   d. Coco the bloody clown. ✓

2. You feel like puking at a murder crime scene. Should you…

   Teach em a lesson!

   a. Aim for the corpse so that you don't have to look at its guts any more? ✗
   b. Aim for the journalists so that they can get some good shots for the evening edition? ✓
   c. Aim for your fellow officers as a laugh? ✗
   d. Sorry? Puke at a crime scene? What are you on about? Why would I? Cast-iron gut, that's me. ✗

3. You've gathered physical evidence. What's your next step?
   a. Talk to informants and interview the public. ✓
   b. Ponce around with physics books and try to come up with silly theories that don't fit the facts. ✗
   c. Gaze into thin air and look gormless for a while. ✗
   d. Smoke fags, throw a paddy, then kick something until it tells you what to do next. ✗

4. What's the best way to pass the time while on a stakeout?
   a. I-spy…or maybe even a quick game of Animal, Vegetable or Mineral. ✓
   b. A lamb bhuna and tandoori naan. ✗
   c. A sing-song. ✗
   d. A game of cards. ✗

5. You're impersonating a train driver while trying to nab a gang of crooks. What do you wear?
   a. A long moustache and furry chaps. ✗
   b. A shiny spacesuit complete with ray gun. ✗
   c. Overalls. ✓
   d. A G-string with titty-tassels. ✗

ANSWERS

1. If you answered...

- a. You think you're Miss Marple.
- b. You think you're James Bond.
- c. You think you're Sherlock Holmes.
- d. You think you're Gene Hunt, well done.

I could be Bond though

2. If you answered...

- a. You're out of a job (and you're nicked for obstructing an investigation).
- b. You're out of a job (and everyone's laughing at you).
- c. You're out of a job (and about to get a good kicking).
- d. You're standing next to me.

oh...

3. If you answered...

- a. You're DCI Gene Hunt.
- b. You're DI Sam Tyler.
- c. You're DC Chris Skelton.
- d. You're DC Ray Carling.

Oi!!!

4. If you answered...

- a. You're definitely something beginning with 'C'.
- b. You better have got me an onion bhaji, too. If so, full marks.
- c. You'll find it hard to sing when I handcuff your lips to the rear-view mirror.
- d. You're busted, pal.

Yeah! Chris!

5. If you answered...

- a. You're so stupid you should do it. Now.
- b. You're not Barbarella, stop being an arse.
- c. You must be a train driver.
- d. You've made my day, Cartwright. Now go get changed.

CHOO! CHOO!

Vice

Sometimes a copper has to get *really* dirty.
Crime isn't all balaclavas and shotguns – sex is a
constant in our cities and there will be plenty of
times when you have to roll up your sleeves and
get in there...

If you know what I mean.

Ahem...

From prostitution to porn, we have a duty to
uphold the laws of moral decency and protect
both the innocent silly minds of the voting public
and those poor sods that get themselves caught
up in it all...

5.1 Prostitution

We all know that this is a mess, but every now and then some eager councillor decides he wants to make a thing of it as he tries to get himself elected (which is a laugh because most of the local council make their second home in the knickers of the hookers they make such a fuss about 'cleaning up'. Perhaps they're just doing research, eh?).

So, things to bear in mind in the world of slap-and-tickle for cash:

a.   Hookers are the best snouts going and any eager copper who thinks they're the encmy is either thick or a poof. Dealing with prostitution is a political game, you need to be seen to be doing something but, at the same time, you want to look after the girls a bit, get 'em on side.

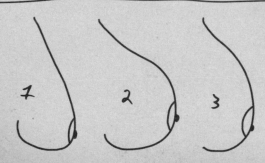

b. Keep these girls off the streets as far as possible. They've got to earn a living but let's encourage them to keep it quiet, eh? You'll find most 'vocal majorities' have less of a problem with the knowledge that prostitution's going on than they do with the fear of their husbands being distracted by the sight of too much leather gusset on their way home from the pub. Get the girls to play the game a bit and the battle's half won.

c. If you do find yourself 'accidentally' being thanked by one of the girls, for God's sake watch yourself. There's more bacteria being shared in this city's alleyways than you'll find in a dead dog's head stuffed with cheese that's been left in the sun for a fortnight. Keep yourself safe and scrub it with a Brillo when you're done.

Body Expert DC Skelton's Guide to Tits

1 – *Droopers, bit boring, seen on older birds*
2 – *Full Pillows – good for face-rubbing*
3 – *Wide Boys – big and wide*

Fig. 5.2 **Men Only.** *Title says it all. It's what this book should be called, too.*

5.2 Porn

The human race is responsible for two of the greatest inventions and forms of expression: the written word and film. When Jeff Kodak (or whoever it was) invented the camera he must have known that one of the main things it would end up pointing at was a cracking pair of tits.

Only natural.

Porn can be split into two easily definable sections:

Softcore: jugs and fur
Hardcore: butcher's shops, spurting and any of that weird animal stuff*

As you know, many of the publications and productions that fit into the hardcore category are illegal, and it's our job as police officers to seize such material when we find it and make sure that nobody *but us* has to watch it...with a few beers and a takeaway.

Bonus!

*I mean, who buys this? Is it for randy farmers or what? If I want to see a donkey's knob I'll go to Blackpool...

Here are some particularly 'shocking' examples that you should make sure you impound if you come across them:

Once Upon a Time in Her Vest
Can't beat a good western, can you? There aren't many guns in this but plenty of shootouts if you catch my drift. The star, Donna Fistful, is a goer too, real hard worker.

The Sexorcist
A few bumps in the night and if National Dairies employed Candi Creamer they'd double their milk output in a year – the girl's got strong arms and a lot of stamina.

Arse Force
Guess what it's about?

Test Yourself on This Section

1. You see a girl 'kerb crawling'. Should you...
    a. Ask her how much? ✓
    b. Tell her to move on or you'll have to give her a hard time? ✗
    c. Run at her with your trousers down and half a pound of butter in your hand? ✗
    d. Book her immediately for being a filthy slut? ✗

2. What is 'softcore'?
    a. A type of road surface. ✗
    b. A waste of time and effort. ✓
    c. Mild porn. ✗
    d. The reason most corner shops stay in business. ✗

3. Where can you get a copy of *Arse Force 2: Do You Feel Mucky, Punk??*
    Who knows?

ANSWERS

1. If you answered...

Yeah! Important, that's me

a.   You're on the local council.

b.   You're a sensible copper (add half a point if you tipped 'er a wink as you said it).

c.   You're Marlon Brando in **Last Tango in Paris** and you put me off **The Godfather** for life, you fat perv.

d.   You're Mary bloody Whitehouse, how did you get in my car?

2. If you answered...

a.   You need to get out more.

b.   You've probably gone blind already, so I'm amazed you managed to read the question.   *Ha!*

c.   You read more than just **Penthouse**.

d.   You've probably got a good point.

3. Wish I knew. If anyone tracks one down, let me know – there's a pint in it for you.

6 Interrogating Suspects

We've all heard the horror stories of over-eager officers putting the boot between the thighs... Ridiculous, and not the sort of thing I'd stand for on my patch. Everyone knows you get better results going for the pressure point in the armpit – easier to apply and you don't have to wait five minutes for the nonce to stop chucking up. Honestly, diving for the man-fruits like a dock-yard slapper – sure sign of an amateur.

There's a time and place for testes and knowing when that is is just another part of learning how to become a better officer. You want good results? Then use your head as well as your fists (and no, I don't mean nut the bastard either). Psychology.

Fig. 6.1.1 Good cop

Fig. 6.1.2 Bad cop

6.1 Getting Them to Talk (Psychological)

You need to play with their heads as well as their nerve endings. We all know the classic good cop/bad cop routine – there's a reason it's famous, too: it gives good results. Still, it's not the only way and there's many simple tricks that play in the same area, so...

a.   I mentioned the clever use of fags earlier (not stubbing them out on your suspect – that can be useful but only as a last resort). When you walk in the room your suspect is on edge, he's tighter than a nun's chuff when the Pope's in town and he's not going to be talking any time soon. Give him a fag. Light it for him. Let him enjoy the relaxing vitamins offered by tobacco for a few seconds. See? He's winding down, starting to think you might be a reasonable bloke, maybe you're even going to let him go in a minute. Don't be afraid to smile either, crack a joke...Look! We're laughing! What good mates we are, settling down for a nice relaxing chat. Now hit him.

b. One of the most important things when messing with a suspect's head is that you never want them to know that you don't know. Do everything you can to give the impression that they are only confirming what you've already heard. This is all part of unsettling them. It makes them suspicious, makes them think about who might have ratted them out. Sow those seeds of distrust cleverly, subtly and intelligently (I find scratching my balls and mentioning that their wife has more crabs than Blackpool front is effective).

c. Imagination is your friend. Sometimes the threat of pain is better than pain itself. When you walk into the interview room say nothing, stare the little bastard out as you calmly place a hammer, a box of toothpicks, three mousetraps, a hacksaw and a large cucumber on the table in front of him. Given a few seconds to imagine how those things could be used, he's likely to be confessing before you've even got your jacket off. Still, if they're lacking imagination it's time for the next section...

6.2 Getting Them to Talk (Physical)

Physical interrogation's a lot like sex – it's all about foreplay and the gradual build. If you immediately weigh in with a boot to the head, where are you going to go from there?

Here's Gene's dance steps to a perfect confession:

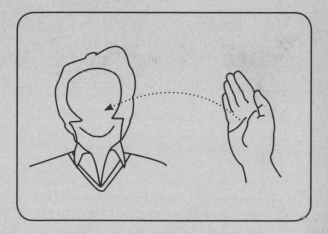

a. <u>The Open-handed Slap</u> (*Fig. 6.2.1*)

It stings and makes a satisfying noise. Mind you, when you've made the sort of suggestions most of us have to the girls around at closing time you'll know that you do get used to the feel of it. So, move on quickly to...

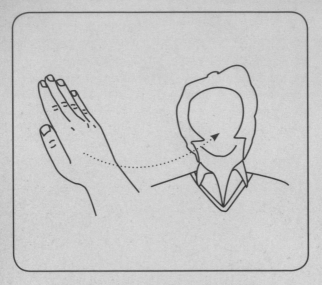

b. **The Back-handed Slap** (*Fig. 6.2.2*)

Much more power, and when you
bring those naughty knuckles (and the
additional possibility of a chunky ring)
into play, the suspect's face is going to
know something's hit it. I've had people
confess after this stage, especially if
you've built in a little whiplash with the
tips of your fingers.

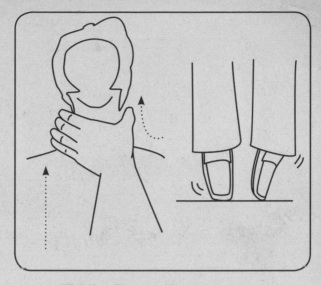

c. <u>**Holding Pattern**</u> (*Fig. 6.2.3*)

Grip them by the throat and lift them just high enough that they have to go on tiptoes. This throws their balance and guarantees that they'll end up parting their legs, leaving their meat and veg dangling and unprotected. (Remember, don't go whacking them there yet, at this point it's about them feeling the swing of freedom and realising that, if you wanted to, you could twist off a knacker with relative ease – a bit more psychology for you).

d. <u>**The Drop**</u> (*Fig. 6.2.4*)

You've lifted them up, now bring them
back down. Yank their head towards the
desk and gravity and their poor balance
will do the rest. The minute their nose
has kissed wood get them back up into
the Holding Pattern again. Repeat until
you get bored.

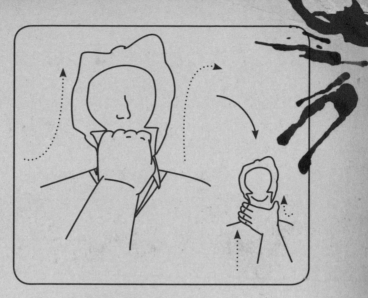

e. <u>**The Back Flip**</u> (*Fig. 6.2.5*)

Now you've had them going up and down
a few times, they're probably starting
to get used to the sensation so it's time
to wrong-foot them again by changing
direction. A straight armed pop to the
nose after pulling them quickly up to the
Holding Pattern will see them on their
arse and shouting.*

* If they're good enough to pull themselves up after this using the
desk (looking like that Chad graffiti – Wot? No Confession?), feel
free to add an extra little smack of their face on wood by pushing
down on the back of their head.

f. <u>**The Casual Chat**</u> (*Fig. 6.2.6*)

Now's the time for a breather, both for
you and for them. When you're getting
thrashed the body does start to give in to
it, and the pain lessens. You need to let
the suspect get back on their feet every
now and then just so there's more effect
when you bring the fists back into play.
Now is also a good time to throw a bit
more of 6.1's psychology in, too. Suspect
still not talking? Then it's time for the
group games...

g. **<u>The Crucifixion</u>** (*Fig. 6.2.7*)

Have your DCs grab an arm each and take the suspect back against the wall. Once pinned against the bricks he should be spread out and defenceless. A simple stab at the kidneys with your fingers in this position will have him writhing. You'll also notice he's ready and accessible for a bit of pit action. Sensitive area, the armpit – just a gentle tickle with the fingertips makes a man squirm. Shoving the thumb in there and twisting will have him shout the roof off. Still not talking? Warm your hands, nurse, we're going in...

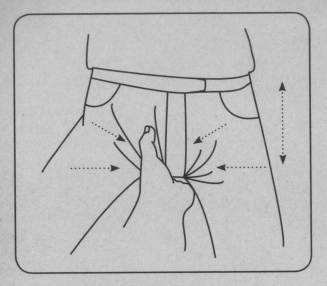

h. <u>**Weighing Up**</u> (*Fig. 6.2.8*)

Many yank the ballsack downwards, but
I'm a fan of the upward tug. It's more
unnatural and, in my experience,
eye-wateringly effective. If he's not
talking now, plums aching, he probably
didn't do it. Best brush him down, pack
him off home and wash your hands. Some
you win, some you lose.

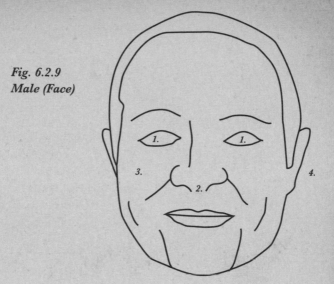

Fig. 6.2.9
Male (Face)

1. <u>**Here's Looking at You**</u> – *The delicate popping of your index and middle fingers here has cracking results.*

2. <u>**Pick Your Own**</u> – *You can lead a blagger to water by pulling here. He'll drink, too. Combine with (1) for 'The Bowling Ball'.*

3. <u>**Cheeky**</u> – *Mind the gob, he'll have your fingers off as surely as a starving Jack Russell would. Yank on his cheeks for a good bit of schoolboy yelping.*

4. <u>**Jug Handles**</u> – *Apparently the ears are not strong enough to support the body's weight, which is all the more reason to try. He'll be screaming the place down before you can say 'Dumbo'.*

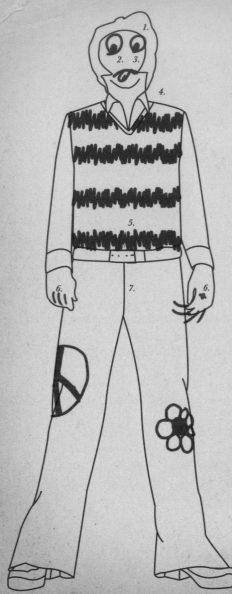

Fig. 6.2.10 Male (Front)

1. _Head_. Not only is it good for tapping against hard surfaces, it's also worth messing with psychologically.

2. _Nose_. Soft place to aim a punch. You'll always hurt them more than you'll hurt yourself.

3. _Cheek_. Slap it.

4. _Throat_. God's handhold for the copper.

5. _Belly_. Another soft landing spot for an officer's fist.

6. These little piggys can easily bend the wrong way!

7. Trust in the power of the _bollock_. If all else fails it's the on/off switch for a confession.

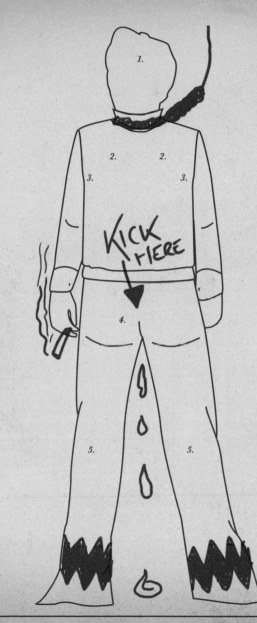

Fig. 6.2.11 Male (Back)

1. Push here to place face in contact with solid object.
2. <u>Shoulderblades</u>. More nice handholds; dig your thumb into the pressure point to sit your suspect down like a good boy.
3. Let's hope he put the Mum on this morning. Get your thumb in his armpit and listen to him sing.
4. No use in an interrogation, but a good place to kick Uniform if you want them to do anything.
5. Press foot here to get your suspect on his knees quickly.

Right, that's enough of all that manliness. Let's take a look at the female figure:

<u>Lovely.</u>

6.3 More Tips for Conducting an Interrogation

a. <u>**When smacking a fag out of a suspect's mouth don't burn your hand.**</u> You're not going to look like the man in charge if you're hopping around blowing on your knuckles now, are you? The trick is to aim for the cheek rather than the gob. Slap 'em hard in the face and the cigarette will fly sure enough.

b. When 'sowing the seeds of distrust' (*see 6.1.b*) <u>**be prepared for the unexpected**</u>. I once had a poor git from Barnsley whip his tackle out and start shouting, 'You think you've got problems? This thing's rotting off!' Turns out his wife did have a dose. The interview did not start on the right foot.

c. <u>**Sometimes physical violence is not reliable.**</u> Some wet ponces will say anything to get you to stop, they may even falsify a confession in order to avoid a kicking. This is not good. Read your suspect, gauge his levels and take it slow.

d. **Know your own limits.** I knew a lad who
    put his back out interviewing a suspect.
    As in *6.3.a*, you don't look in control if
    you're rolling on the floor asking for a
    nurse yourself. If you're not up to the job
    get in someone else who is.

e. I once had the misfortune to end up
    interrogating a kinky old sod who
    thought his birthday had come early. It
    was only when I got to the 'Weighing Up'
    and realised I had a hold on something
    heavier than normal did I cotton on to
    the fact that the bastard was enjoying
    himself. Turns out he had nothing to
    do with the case in question but had a
    history of putting himself up as a false
    suspect hoping for a professional
    going-over. I booked him for wasting
    police time then went and got drunk.
    Never have I felt so used.

Test Yourself on This Section

And you know that I can make you answer them too...

1. Pick two items you could use to intimidate a suspect:
    a.   A shotgun and an axe. ✓
    b.   A begonia and Shredded Wheat. ✗
    c.   Garlic and a crucifix. ✗
    d.   A mousetrap and a hammer. ✗

2. When should you grab a man's balls?
    a.   As a last resort when he won't talk. ✓
    b.   The minute he walks through the door, tugging them like you're ringing church bells. ✗
    c.   Whenever he asks you to... ✗
    d.   When he's a high-ranking police officer who has entered the bar you're standing in (in genuine ignorance of what sort of establishment it actually is). ✗

3. If someone tries to complain about their treatment during an interrogation you should...
    a.   Smile gently and reach for the hammer so they think twice before pushing their luck ✓
    b.   Run panicking to your Guv.
    c.   Shoot them in the head twice and then dump the body in the canal. ✗
    d.   Beg them to torture you as fair punishment. ✗

ANSWERS

1. If you answered...

a. You're John Wayne. *the Duke – that's me!*

b. You're Spike Milligan.

c. You're Peter Cushing.

d. You're Gene Hunt.

2. If you answered...

a. You're getting there. *got it right.*

b. You're my wife and I wasn't even that pissed.

c. You're not my wife but I wish you were...

d. You're that handlebar-moustached bastard from last Friday and if I see you again I'll do more than pop you on the nose. Ask before you touch, pal.

3. If you answered...

a. You're getting the hang of the psychology. *yeah. i'm gettin it.*

b. You'll get a slap of your own from me the minute you step into the office for being a pansy.

c. You're that nutter Harry West from F Division and you were bound to get caught.

d. You know who you are and so do I – so pack it in before I mention names, you stupid kink.

7 Staff Relations

A DCI gets nowhere without his people behind him – a sheriff needs his deputies. One of the most important parts of police work is sticking by your fellow officers.

Also, in these enlightened times, it's vital you know how to work with the fairer sex. It's difficult to talk to them of course, it's all hairstyles, perfume and Donny bloody Osmond. Still, blank all that out, heap on the charm and you might just get somewhere.

Finally, it's important to know how to deal with those upstairs…the men whose job it is to worry about what they keep calling 'the big picture' (usually meaning the press or their pension). Politics…hate it, but you have to know how to play the game.

Fig. 7.1.a

Fig. 7.1.b

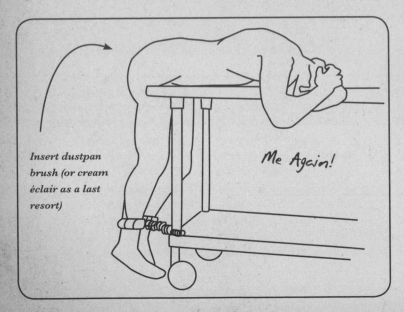

Insert dustpan
brush (or cream
éclair as a last
resort)

Me Again!

Fig. 7.1.c

7.1 Dealing with the Rest of Your Team

a. **Stand your round.** Nobody likes a sponger or a dry mouth.

b. **Crash the fags.** Smoking's important, a group sport, so always be ready with a Player and a light when you arrive at the crime scene. Fags help you think: scientific fact.

c. A piss-take is one thing but **always know where to draw the line.** A certain amount of horseplay is vital, blows off steam and builds morale, but if you let it get out of control then everything can go tits up. Example: a young detective in my unit celebrated his birthday by being tied naked to a tea trolley and wheeled through the girls' changing rooms. Nobody minded, all a good laugh, but to top it off somebody tried to stick a cream éclair up his jacksy. Ridiculous. It was a step too far and a waste of a cake. We settled on a dustpan brush instead. Funnier, less sticky and an extra surprise for the cleaners when they called in the morning. Double the laugh – compromise and common sense.

d. <u>Say what you mean.</u> I've no time for people who waffle – life's too short. Straight talking, always the best way.

e. <u>Stand by your boys.</u> We all make mistakes now and then – I can't quite remember the last time *I* did to be honest, but I'm sure it's happened once or twice – and it's important that you rally round when it happens. Keep your own house clean. If somebody steps out of line and causes a problem, deal with it yourself without calling in the boys from upstairs. Trust, it goes both ways.

Fig. 7.2.d Hell hath no fury, and all that.

7.2 Dealing with Female Officers

a. **Never forget the power of a firm palm on the right plonk's arse.** A little smack and the whiff of Brut up their nostrils knocks 'em bandy, and you'll never be short changed on the custard creams again. Girls like to be appreciated.

b. **Hold a door open for them once in a while.** It may be old-fashioned but it all helps to make them feel a bit special (and the reward is the view of their behind as you walk after them).

c. **Take them seriously.** I know they have a head full of candyfloss and hairspray most days but sometimes you can learn about the female motive, which is helpful. Plus they love it when you listen. Look the sensitive sort and you'll have your Y-fronts off before you can say 'modern man'.

d. **Watch the calendar.** Keep your eyes peeled for the signs as there's no point in trying to get a straight answer from them when the decorators are in.

7.3 Dealing with Superiors

Unlike Uniform, we CID officers don't need a series of badges on our shoulders to know who's in charge. For the particularly dense, here is a brief rundown, in **ascending** order of rank:

yeah. I'm at the top. most important.

Detective Constable (DC)
Detective Sergeant (DS)
Detective Inspector (DI)
Detective Chief Inspector (DCI – aka Me)
Detective Superintendent
Detective Chief Superintendent

The last two like to think they're important, so they don't get initials like us lucky lot. As for dealing with them:

a. The voice from above says you have to keep your nose clean, play it straight. Get it through your head that this means you have to *appear* **clean and straight** – there's a big difference.

b. **Get on good drinking terms with them.** Some of them are *you* given a few years and some lucky breaks (let's ignore those university rank-jumpers, shall we?). If the superintendent's your mate, life is easier. If that doesn't work…

c.   **Even out the field.** It's worth knowing a few things about your bosses – what casinos, golf courses or strip joints they frequent. **Knowledge is power.** If *they* know that *you* know plenty about them they won't be in any rush to force your hand, will they? Basic poker strategy.

d.   They'll tell you that you have to be careful about the press and/or the public. This is *not* true. Your job is to catch criminals, not worry about the Force looking good in the papers. Public Relations is *their* job and they just want to make life easier for themselves by delegating. If you make a mess it's their job to tidy it up. It's why they have the big houses and motors; let them earn both.

e.   **Tell them as little as you can during an investigation.** Give them an inch and they'll take a mile – you mention a name and before you know it some bastard's announced a press conference. Keep them in the dark, keep them off your back. They'll find out what they need to know when it's all over.

f.   None of the above refer to your DCI. Your DCI is god and he has rules all of his own…

7.4 Dealing with the Guv (Me)

a. Tea, two sugars.

b. Bourbons, you ponce, you can stick your Rich Tea.

c. Get your bloody hands off my Scotch.

d. <u>Seriously</u>, touch my Scotch and I'll kneecap you.

Fig. 7.4 Me letting someone admire my Scotch. I may even let him sniff the glass if he's been a good boy.

Test Yourself on This Section

1. Gis a fag.
   a. Of course, Guv. Here, let me light it for you. ✓
   b. Sorry, Guv, I don't smoke. ✗
   c. Get your own, Guv, I've only a couple left. ✗
   d. Do you like menthol? ✗

2. How many sugars do I take?
   a. None. ✗
   b. One. ✗
   c. Two. ✓
   d. Three. ✗

3. Is that my Scotch in your hand?
   a. No, Guv. ✓
   b. No, Guv. ✓
   c. No, Guv. ✓
   d. No, Guv. ✓

ANSWERS

1. If you answered…

   a.   You're a star.
   b.   You're a tit.
   c.   You're a bastard.
   d.   I'm not even **talking** to you.

correct.
1 point.

2. If you answered…

   a.   You must be my doctor.
   b.   You're not listening.
   c.   You must be Cartwright. God bless you (and all
       who sail in you), darling.
   d.   You saying I'm fat?

correct.
another 1 point.

3. If you answered a), b), c) or d)…

   It better not have bloody been.

correct.
4 points.

6/3

8 Off Duty

We all know the job can take over. We wake up, run around after some crooked bastard all day long, then fall asleep again. It's no good, every copper needs time to forget about the job for a bit.

When you've had a day full of clues and bruises you need somewhere to go so that your brain can take it all in and make sense of it.

That place is, of course, the pub.

Fig. 8.1.b Ambrosia

Fig. 8.1.c The drink of champions

Fig. 8.1.d Unacceptable alternatives

8.1 Socialising

A really good pub is an amazing place. Don't be fooled into thinking that every dump with a pint in it is worth making your local. There are a few things that every bloke needs to make sure of before he graces the stool with his arse:

a. <u>Jukebox.</u> Now, I can be happy without any music frankly. I listen to suspects sing all day, so it's nice to have a bit of peace, but if you *must* have a jukebox then make sure it's not rammed full of the sort of bollocks that'll have you beating it to death with your barstool within five minutes. Ballroom *bloody* Blitz? Gary *sodding* Glitter? It's like having a minced dog turd rubbed in your ears.

b. <u>Decent beer.</u> (*See Fig. 8.1.b.*) Lager is not fit to wash your balls in and doesn't count.

c. When you run out of room for the beer it's also good to know the barman has a <u>good Scotch</u> to pour in you. (*See Fig. 8.1.c.*)

d. Beer and Scotch are the *only* types of alcohol recognised by a real man. Wine is a ladies' drink, named after the noise they frequently make. Brandy is a type of medicine dispensed by dogs.

e. **No fruit machines.** If I want to 'hold the melons and nudge', I'll do so in private and with the woman of my choice, thank you.

f. **Plenty of good table space.** Pubs and poker go hand in hand – you want to make sure you have a bit of elbow room.

g. **A relaxed attitude towards closing time.** There's nothing worse than being a copper and having the bloody law quoted at *you*.

Railway Arms 'Dome of Stars' Drinking Competition
– loser buys all drinks

Ray	IIII II\	pints
ME	II	pints (+ 1 babysham)
		– i GOT there LATE
Gerald	IIII II	pints
The Guv	IIII IIII II	pints,
	III\	WHISKYS
Annie	IIII	red wine
Sam	II\	pints (AND A RED WINE – PONCE)

RAY WOZ HERE

8.2 Alternatives

Just in case there's something deeply wrong with you and you would like an alternative to the pub once in a while, here are a few personal recommendations in the Manchester area:

a. <u>**Two of a Kind**</u>
Pinborough Street, M1
Nice little casino with a bar priced just beneath the need to get a mortgage to keep drinking. Not for those whose card-playing ability is 'Beggar My Neighbour' and 'Happy Families' though – the clientele are a canny bunch. Mind you, if I'm playing then feel free to join in, I'll be happy to show you where you're going wrong.

b. <u>Jump and Jiggle</u>
Ferguson Road, M3
A select little nightclub where the music is rough but the girls make Olga Korbut look like a paraplegic.

c. <u>The Gentlemen's Relish</u>
Parker Lane, M2
I couldn't possibly recommend that you visit this filthy establishment. I also couldn't suggest you ask for Sarah or Rebecca when you arrange your evening's entertainment. I really couldn't mention it being worth the extra to have both of them perform the 'wheelbarrow' with you either despite it being damn good value and the most shocking thing you'll see outside of Bangkok. Honestly. I couldn't do any of those things. (Avoid Fridays, Sarah knocks off early.)

d. <u>The Daisy Cup</u>
Gale Street, M2
A lovely little teashop that does dances in the evenings and a free slice of fruitcake with every cup of tea. And that's what you are if you think I'm being serious: a bloody fruitcake. Go to the pub. Now.

Test Yourself on This Section

1. What's a Harvey Wallbanger?
   a. A back-alley male prostitute. ✗
   b. A drink made from vodka, orange juice and Galliano. ✗
   c. How the bloody hell should I know? Not beer or whisky, is it? ✓
   d. You're my best friend you are. ✗

2. If you've got a 'royal flush' you have…?
   a. A gold handle on your lav. ✗
   b. A sweat on from walking the corgis. ✗
   c. Probably won your hand of poker. ✓
   d. Put ointment on it and are hoping it'll get better soon. ✗

3. What's a 'one-armed bandit'?
   a. A wounded Mexican. ✓
   b. A lazy poof. ✗
   c. An annoying bastard thing in the middle of a pub. ✗
   d. A sure way of winning a few quid. ✗

ANSWERS

1. If you answered…

a.   You're nothing to do with me.

b.   You're wearing a frock.

c.   <u>Your round I think.</u>

d.   You've had enough.

another one right. 7 point.

2. If you answered…

a.   What can I get you, Superintendent?

b.   Good evening, Your Majesty. What will it be?

c.   <u>The drinks are on you.</u>

d.   Have you touched my pint? Go and wash your hands.

and again! Skelton's on a roll. 7 point.

3. If you answered…

a.   You need to get out more.

b.   Don't go out ever again, I might bump into you.

c.   Jackpot.

d.   Remind me to play cards with you some time, you're a pushover.

shut up!

9 External Relations and Complaints

Sometimes in this job you have to deal with the public or press which is never a good thing – outside the examples quoted in Section 4 when using the public or press is a necessary evil – because it always boils down to the inevitable complaints and whinging.

Policemen make enemies, we're whipping boys for the public and good column inches for the hacks. Sometimes we have to get our hands dirty, which usually ends up with noses out of joint and complaint forms on your desk. Time spent dealing with that is time wasted. So, here's one final section of advice for when you're asked to justify your actions.

9.1 Dealing with Complaints

a. Tell 'em to fuck off.

Fig. 9.1 Yeah, you heard.

Appendix One
Looking the Part

'Clothes make the man', as Shakespeare probably said (haven't got the matchbox I read it off to hand to be honest), and he was right.

You don't get any respect for turning up at a crime scene looking like your mum dressed you funny – that's half the nation's CID in trouble already.

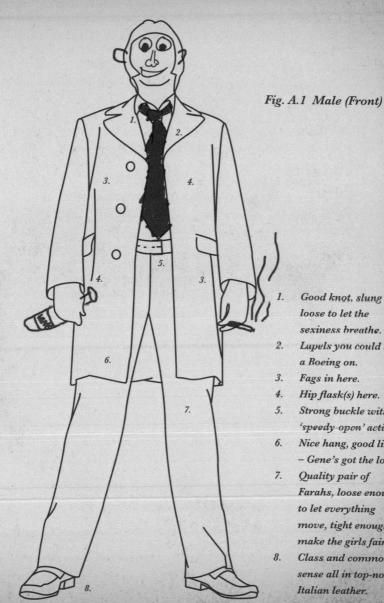

Fig. A.1 Male (Front)

1. Good knot, slung loose to let the sexiness breathe.
2. Lapels you could land a Boeing on.
3. Fags in here.
4. Hip flask(s) here.
5. Strong buckle with 'speedy-open' action.
6. Nice hang, good lines – Gene's got the look.
7. Quality pair of Farahs, loose enough to let everything move, tight enough to make the girls faint.
8. Class and common sense all in top-notch Italian leather.

Obviously if you're Uniform there's nothing you can do about this but then again what do the old biddies care about your togs when you're fishing their cats out of trees, eh? For the rest of you it's very simple:

a. Get a **good suit.** Plenty of crease and lapels that you could cut your fingers on.

b. **Decent shirt with a good collar.** Avoid patterns for God's sake – flouncing about like a fairy in a shirt made out of curtains will only get you pegged as a nonce.

c. Top it off with a **good tie.** For those of you that don't know how to tie a decent knot then make it like a noose, slip it over your head and yank hard – you shouldn't have left home and you're no use to me. Mind you, a clip-on has its advantages – just watch a slag's face when they grab hold of *that* in a fight and it comes off in their hands!

d. **Slip-on shoes.** They show class and you're never going to go arse over tit during a foot pursuit cos your lace is undone.

e. **A good overcoat** isn't essential but it does polish off the image and offers extra storage for your fags, hip flask and other items *(see 1.1).*

Simple Advice for Plod

It's been suggested that I haven't given enough constructive advice for the lower ranks so I'm forced to try and come up with some woodentop-friendly pointers to keep everyone happy.

We've all been there, I suppose – some for longer than others though, eh?

helmet

Here are the Guv's handy pointers for our little friends in Uniform:

a. *Dixon of Dock Green* is not a documentary, now stop crying.

b. Twenty per cent of the regional uniform division suffered some form of light injury last year (splinters from their pencils, cat scratches during rescue missions, scalded mouths from too many rushed cups of tea, that sort of thing). Yes, you can get yourself in dangerous situations, stop whinging.

c. Riots really *are* dangerous...seen my fair share, haven't I? Couldn't swear to how brave the boys in blue were (they were behind me most of the time while I was bashing heads with my broom handle) but I'm sure they dealt with any stragglers I missed.

d. When I say to keep a crowd of spectators under control I *mean* it...I've watched you lot, wandering around waving your arms and daydreaming about pie in the canteen. *People still get through.* I sometimes wonder if it would be better to ask the public if they could look after *you*.

e. Don't go all doe-eyed over Plonks! You'd think you'd never seen a woman in uniform. Besides, everybody knows that the girls prefer detectives…

f. A whistle! Ha!

g. Do yourself a favour. If you're out on duty (messing about on your bike no doubt) and you see a beautiful copper-coloured Ford Cortina Mark III (2000E*…oh *yes*)** heading towards you at what you suspect to be above the speed limit, put your helmet over your face, count to five and when you look again I'll be out of your way. Do not, under any circumstances, try and pull me over. I am probably in high pursuit and saving lives like the hero I am. Even if I'm not I'll have a damn good reason – and yes, Constable Mark Morris, Badge Number 491, getting home while my tikka masala's still bubbling *is* a good reason *whatever* you tried to imply to the contrary last week, you miserable little skinhead.

h. Get promoted, then I'll stop picking on you.

* The 'E' stands for 'executive' – even my car has a better rank than you.

** Licence Number KJM 212K. Remember it, name your bloody kids after it, I want that number etched on your little brain.

Appendix Three
Glossary

Like any other job, being a copper comes with its own language (some of it rude enough to kill the Pope just by listening).

You can't expect to get anywhere without being understood or, come to that, understanding what everyone's saying to you.

Aggro	Aggravation – what I'll give you if you don't follow every rule in here to the letter.
'Arris	Your arse – the thing you need to get off now that you've finally finished the book.
Bird	*See* Dolly-Bird
Blag	Payroll robbery
Blagger	Come on, don't be thick.
Cooper, Gary	God amongst men.
Crooks	The blokes that keep us employed (criminals that is, not the Chief Super. Mind you, now I come to think about it…).
Dabs	Fingerprints
Dixon of Dock Green	*See Z Cars*
Dolly-Bird	*See* Quim
'Er Indoors	The reason I work long hours.
Fag	Health food enjoyed by real men.
Fairy	Man United supporter.
Fit Up	I think it's something to do with falsifying evidence. That's what I heard anyway…
Form	Criminal record

Grass	Informant
Guv	Me, the Governor
Hooker	Prostitute or Welshman confused about football
Intuition	What I've got and you haven't – otherwise you wouldn't need this book.
Job	A robbery, and what I'm doing when I nab the bastards for doing it.
Keks	Y-fronts
Lag, Old	Someone who's done plenty of time in prison.
MO	Modus operandi. Latin for the way people operate.
Nab	Catch
Nonce	Sex offender
Off Duty	When you don't have to worry about walking straight when you leave the pub.
Plod	Uniform police
Plonk	Police(*cough*)woman
Ponce	A girly bloke
Porkies	Pork pies...lies. Southern ponce rhyming slang.

Porn	Both work *and* a hobby.
Porridge	Prison sentence
Previous	'Previous form' – criminal record
Quim	*See* Skirt (or what you might find *in* one…nudge nudge)
Rules	Made to be broken
Scotch	What you buy the Guv whenever you like. Single, mind you, none of that blended crap.
Scrote	As in 'scrotum' – the sack where a man holds 'is brains
Shooter	Gun or the bloke holding it
Skirt	*See* Bird
Slag	Petty criminal or slapper
Slapper	*See* Tart
Snout	Informant
Stitch Up	*See* Fit Up
Stretch	Prison sentence
Tart	*See* Slapper
Tit	A lovely natural invention and an idiot
Uniform	Poor sods who aren't clever enough to be proper coppers yet

Vagina	Nice
Woodentop	Uniform police
Xylophone	The only thing I can think of that starts with 'x'
Y-fronts	Meat holster
Z-Cars	What Plod thinks of as 'real life'.

DC Chris Skelton	Genius copper, love god, martial arts GRAND MASTER, sharp shooter, takes his beer like a real man, love god

About the Author
DCI Gene Hunt

DCI Gene Hunt is a long-serving member of the North-West District CID.

DCI Gene Hunt is watching you, and if you don't do your job properly he'll come round your house and set fire to you while you're sleeping.

'You're an overweight, over-the-hill, nicotine-stained, borderline alcoholic homophobe with a superiority complex and an unhealthy obsession with male bonding.'
– DC Sam Tyler (who sometimes says the sweetest things)

A few boys and girls got going with their Box brownies. These are the people we had to convince in order to reproduce the pictures. Most of them were fine about it but needed walking through the interrogation section before signing the forms. You get me?

Lee Thompson – p. 22, p. 23, p. 48, p. 70
Jason Antony – p. 32 (3.2.1, original image)
Matt Gant – p. 38 (4.1.b), p. 105, p. 114 (9.1), p. 127
Bazil Raubach – p. 106 (8.1.d)
Peter van der Rol – p. 106 (8.1.c)
Michal Zacharzewski –p. 106 (8.1.b)
Matt Wood @ 3sixtymedia – p. 109 (Original Image)
Dave Gilligan – p. 122

Images on p. 70 and p. 90 are property of Paul Raymond Publications Ltd.